# Exploring Best Spanish Wine and Food Pairings

Linsley Ashley

# TABLE OF CONTENT

# CHAPTER ONE

## Introduction to Spanish Cuisine and Wine

Spain is one of the world's most popular tourist destinations, and one of the reasons for this is its rich gastronomic culture. Spanish food reflects the country's rich history, geography, and climate, and it has something for everyone's taste and preference. Furthermore, Spain is home to many world-renowned wine areas that produce some of the world's greatest wines. This chapter will present an overview of Spanish food and wine culture, as well as prominent ingredients and flavors, as well as the many wine regions in Spain.

## Cuisine from Spain

The variety, color, and flavor of Spanish food are well-known. It is influenced by the country's rich history and geography, with culinary traditions influenced by Roman, Arab, and Jewish traditions. Because Spain has a long coastline, seafood plays an important role in the country's cuisine. Furthermore, the country has a warm climate, so fruits and vegetables are plentiful and fresh.

Olives, almonds, garlic, saffron, paprika, and tomatoes are some of the most popular Spanish ingredients. Cured meats, such as chorizo and serrano ham, are very popular in Spanish cuisine. Paella, a rice-based meal with fish or pork, gazpacho, a cold soup prepared with tomatoes and cucumbers, and tortilla espaola, a potato omelet, are among popular foods.

Tapas, or tiny dishes of food served with drinks, are another feature of Spanish cuisine. Tapas began in Andalusia, Spain's southernmost region, and have since spread throughout the country. Patatas bravas, fried potatoes with a spicy tomato sauce, and croquetas, small fried balls of bechamel sauce with various fillings, are two of the most popular tapas dishes.

## Wines from Spain

After Italy and France, Spain is the world's third-largest wine-producing country. It has a long winemaking tradition that dates back to the Roman Empire. Spain has more vineyard acreage than any other country on the planet, and it boasts more than 70 wine regions.

Rioja, Ribera del Duero, Priorat, and Ras Baixas are some of Spain's most well-known wine areas. Rioja is Spain's largest and most famous wine region, located in the country's north. It is well-known for producing high-quality Tempranillo red wines. Ribera del Duero is another well-known wine region in northern Spain that is recognized for its full-bodied red wines created from the Tempranillo grape. Priorat is a tiny wine region in Catalonia recognized for producing high-quality red wines from old vines. Ras Baixas is a white wine region in Galicia famed for its crisp, refreshing Albario grape-based wines.

Spanish wine is famous for its variety, with a vast variety of grape varietals and wine styles. Tempranillo, Garnacha, Monastrell, and Albario are some of the most popular grape varietals in Spain. Many Spanish wines are aged in oak barrels for several years before being released, demonstrating their aging potential.

Finally, Spanish food and wine culture reflect the country's varied history, geography, and climate. The variety, color, and flavor of Spanish cuisine are well known, with seafood playing an important role in the country's culinary tradition. Spanish wine is also noted for its variety, having a diverse selection of grape varietals and wine styles. Spain has many world-renowned wine areas that produce some of the world's finest wines. In the next chapters, we will look at the various wine and food pairings that contribute to the popularity of Spanish cuisine and wine culture.

# CHAPTER TWO

## Basics of Wine Tasting and Pairing

Wine tasting and pairing can be frightening subjects for individuals who are new to the wine world. However, this is not required. In this chapter, we'll go over the fundamentals of wine tasting and pairing, such as how to properly taste wine, the many varieties of wine and their qualities, and how to combine wine with food.

## Wine Tasting Techniques

Wine tasting entails evaluating the attributes of a wine using your senses of sight, smell, and taste. The basic processes for tasting wine are as follows:

**Take a look at the wine:** Begin by inspecting the wine in your glass. Note the viscosity, clarity, and color.

**Examine the wine:** Swirl the wine in your glass to release the aromas, then hold it up to your nose and inhale deeply. Try to identify the aromas of the wine, such as fruit, spice, or wood.

Take a small sip of the wine and hold it on your tongue for a few seconds before swallowing. Take note of the wine's flavor profile, which includes its sweetness, acidity, and tannins.

**Examine the wine:** Consider how the wine tastes and how you feel about it after tasting it. Take into account its balance, complexity, and overall quality.

## Wine Types and Their Characteristics

There are numerous sorts of wine, each with its own distinct features. Among the most popular types of wine are:

**Red wine:** Made from dark grapes, red wine is recognized for its full-bodied flavor and tannins. Cabernet Sauvignon, Pinot Noir, and Merlot are popular red wine varieties.

**White wine:** Made from light-colored grapes, white wine is noted for its crisp, refreshing flavor. Chardonnay,

Sauvignon Blanc, and Riesling are popular white wine varieties.

**Rosé wine:** Rosé wine is a light, fruity wine made from a combination of red and white grapes. Rosé wines can be pale pink to deep pink in color.

Sparkling wine is a carbonated wine that is popular for its effervescent texture and joyful attitude. Champagne is a popular sparkling wine, but there are many other options, such as Prosecco and Cava.

Fortified wine is wine that has been fortified with spirits such as brandy to boost its alcohol concentration. Fortified wines include, among others, Madeira, Port, and Sherry.

### Wine and Food Combination

Finding complimentary or contrasting flavors that improve both the food and the wine is the goal of wine pairing. The following are some general rules for wine and food pairing:

**Match the ferocity:** Light-bodied wines go well with lighter foods, while full-bodied wines go well with heavier foods.

**Consider the following flavors**: Wines should be paired with dishes that have complementing flavors. A fruity white wine, for example, goes well with shellfish, but a full-bodied red wine goes well with red meat.

**Take a look at the acidity:** To balance the flavors, pair acidic wines with acidic foods.

**Consider the following:** To balance the flavors, pair sweet wines with desserts or spicy dishes.

### Cuisine from Spain.

### Wine and Spanish Cuisine Pairing

Spain is well-known for its rich culinary traditions, which include intense flavors and a wide variety of ingredients. There are various elements to consider when matching wine with Spanish cuisine.

Consider the region from whence the food originated first. Spain has numerous wine areas, each with their own distinct varietals and flavor profiles. If you're eating a dish from Catalonia, you might wish to combine it with a local red wine, such as a Priorat or a Montsant.

Consider the major elements in the recipe next. Spanish cuisine frequently includes shellfish, cured meats, and substantial stews, all of which complement various varieties of wine. Consider matching fish meals with a crisp white wine, such as Albario or Verdejo. A robust red wine, such as Tempranillo or Garnacha, goes well with preserved foods. A full-bodied red wine, such as Rioja or Ribera del Duero, will stand up well to the rich flavors of robust stews.

Finally, consider the dish's overall flavor profile. The use of robust spices and herbs, such as paprika, saffron, and garlic, is characteristic of Spanish cuisine. Look for wines with similar flavor profiles when matching these dishes with wine. A paprika-seasoned dish, for example, may match well with a Rioja with smokey wood characteristics.

Finally, when done correctly, wine tasting and pairing can be a fun and rewarding experience. You can begin to explore the world of wine with confidence by following the fundamental procedures for tasting wine and understanding the different varieties of wine and their qualities. Consider the area, major components, and overall flavor profile of the dish when matching wine with Spanish food to find complementary or contrasting flavors that improve both. In the next chapters, we will look at specific wine and food pairings that complement various types of Spanish cuisine.

# CHAPTER THREE

## White Wines and Seafood Pairings

Seafood is a popular ingredient in Spanish cooking, with dishes ranging from simple grilled fish to elaborate paellas stuffed with a variety of shellfish. White wines are frequently the best choice for pairing with shellfish. We'll look at some of the greatest white wines to combine with Spanish seafood meals in this chapter.

### Albariño

Albario is a light-bodied white wine cultivated in northwest Spain's Ras Baixas region. This wine is noted for its sharp acidity and lemony aromas, making it an excellent match for seafood recipes. Albario pairs particularly well with seafood dishes such as clams, mussels, and scallops. The acidity of the wine cuts through the richness of the shellfish, and the lemony aromas give a pleasant counterpoint.

Verdejo is another light-bodied white wine grown mostly in north-central Spain's Rueda region. This wine is noted for its flowery aromas and sharp acidity, making it an excellent match for seafood recipes. Verdejo pairs particularly nicely with white fish dishes like cod and hake. The floral notes of the wine match the delicate tastes of the fish, while the acidity cuts through any thick sauces or buttery preparations.

Godello is a medium-bodied white wine grown mostly in northwest Spain's Valdeorras region. This wine is noted for its fruity aromas and mineral undertones, making it an excellent match for marine recipes. Godello pairs particularly nicely with oily fish dishes like salmon and tuna. The wine's fruity notes enhance the fish's strong flavors, while its mineral undertones give a welcome contrast.

**Txakoli**

Txakoli is a light-bodied white wine grown primarily in northern Spain's Basque Country. This wine is noted for its effervescence and acidity, making it an excellent match for seafood recipes. Txakoli pairs very well with grilled or fried fish, such as sardines and anchovies. The wine's effervescence contrasts nicely with the smokey notes of the fish, and its acidity cuts through any heavy sauces or oily preparations.

## White Wines to Pair with Spanish Seafood Dishes

Let's look at some particular pairings now that we've covered some of the best white wines to pair with Spanish seafood meals.

### Octopus grilled with Albario

Grilled octopus is a traditional Spanish dish that consists of delicate, smoky octopus with potatoes and paprika. This dish goes well with Albario, which enhances the smokey tastes of the octopus while offering a refreshing counterpoint to the dish's richness.

**Clams with Verdejo Green Sauce**

Clams in green sauce is a traditional Spanish meal made with clams in a garlic and parsley sauce. Verdejo enhances the delicate flavors of the clams while cutting through the richness of the sauce in this dish.

**Salmon with Godello sauce**

Grilled salmon is a traditional Spanish dish that consists of creamy, buttery fish with vegetables and a white wine sauce. This dish goes well with Godello, which enhances the fruity aromas of the salmon while giving a refreshing counterpoint to the dish's richness.

**Txakoli-encrusted anchovies**

Fried anchovies are a traditional Spanish dish that consists of crispy, salty anchovies served with lemon and parsley. This meal goes well with Txakoli, which gives a refreshing contrast to the anchovies' salty, smokey aromas.

White Wine Pairing Suggestions for Spanish Seafood Dishes

There are a few things to keep in mind when matching white wines with Spanish seafood dishes:

**Consider the following preparation method:** Different methods of cooking can bring out different flavors in seafood dishes. Grilled or fried seafood, for example, may have a smoky or burnt flavor, whereas seafood in a sauce may be rich and creamy. When selecting a white wine to pair with the dish, keep the preparation method in mind.

**Consider the weight of the wine:** White wines differ in body from light to full-bodied, and the weight of the wine can influence how well it matches with food. Lighter-bodied wines, such as Albario and Txakoli, match well with delicate seafood dishes, whilst fuller-bodied wines, such as Chardonnay, can handle heavier seafood dishes.

**Consider the wine's acidity:** White wine's acidity can help to cut through the richness of seafood dishes, making it an excellent match for meals with buttery sauces or fatty preparations. Wines with strong acidity, such as Albario and Txakoli, are ideal for pairing with fish meals.

**Don't be frightened to try new things:** While there are some classic white wine pairings with Spanish seafood dishes, don't be afraid to try new combinations. Wine tasting is an individual experience, and everyone's palate is unique. To find fresh and fascinating flavor combinations, try different white wines with different seafood meals.

Finally, when it comes to wine pairing with Spanish seafood meals, white wines are an excellent choice. Wines like Albario, Verdejo, Godello, and Txakoli are noted for their sharp acidity, fruity aromas, and mineral undertones, making them ideal for a range of seafood recipes. Consider the cooking process, the weight and acidity of the wine, and don't be afraid to explore to discover new and intriguing flavor combinations when matching white wine with seafood.

# CHAPTER FOUR

## Red Wines and Meat Pairings

Spain is famous for its robust and savory meats, which include luscious beef, delicate lamb, and rich pork. When it comes to matching these meats with red wine, there are numerous alternatives. In this chapter, we'll look at some of Spain's most popular red wine and meat combos.

## Pairings of Tempranillo with Beef

Tempranillo is a well-known and commonly planted grape variety in Spain. It is well-known for its full-bodied character, which includes robust tannins and flavors of black cherry, leather, and tobacco. Tempranillo pairs well with beef meals like steak or beef stew because the tannins in the wine cut through the richness of the meat and accentuate its robust flavor.

## Lamb with Garnacha Pairings

Garnacha, often known as Grenache, is a red grape variety grown extensively in Spain. Its flavor profile is fruity and spicy, with overtones of red fruit, cinnamon, and clove. Garnacha pairs well with lamb meals like roast lamb or lamb chops because the wine's fruity flavors enhance the natural sweetness of the lamb.

## Pork and Monastrell Pairings

Monastrell, often known as Mourvèdre, is a grape variety produced in Spain's Mediterranean region. It is well-known for its full-bodied flavor, which includes black fruit, black pepper, and tobacco. Monastrell pairs well with pork meals like pork chops or roast pork because the wine's strong flavor enhances the rich richness of the meat.

## Other Red Wine and Meat Combinations

There are many additional red wines that combine nicely with Spanish meat recipes besides Tempranillo,

Garnacha, and Monastrell. Cabernet Sauvignon, for example, pairs well with beef meals like beef stew or roast beef because the wine's robust tannins enhance the richness of the meat. Syrah is another red wine that goes well with Spanish meat dishes like lamb or venison because the wine's spicy and peppery qualities complement the meat's strong flavor.

**Red Wine Pairing Suggestions for Spanish Meat Dishes**

There are a few things to keep in mind when matching red wines with Spanish meat dishes:

**Consider the wine's weight:** The weight of the wine, like that of white wines, can influence how it matches with food. Full-bodied wines like Tempranillo and Monastrell match well with rich and substantial meat meals, but lighter-bodied wines like Garnacha pair well with more delicate meat dishes.

**Consider the following preparation method:** The method of preparation of the meat dish might also influence the combination. Meats that have been grilled or roasted may have a smokey flavor, whereas slow-cooked meats may have a more complex and layered flavor. When selecting a red wine to combine with the dish, keep the preparation process in mind.

**Take a look at the seasoning:** The seasoning of the meat dish may also have an impact on the match. A severely spiced dish, for example, may overpower a delicate wine, but a wine with powerful flavors can stand up to a heavily seasoned dish.

**Don't be frightened to try new things:** Experiment with different red wines and meat meals to uncover new and fascinating flavor combinations, just like you would with white wine pairings.

Finally, many red wines pair well with Spanish meat dishes, such as Tempranillo, Garnacha, Monastrell, Cabernet Sauvignon, and Syrah. Consider the weight and preparation method of the dish, as well as the seasoning and flavors involved, when matching red wine with meat. By considering these parameters, you may achieve ideal harmony between the wine and the meat, boosting the overall dining experience.

When it comes to wine and food pairings, keep in mind that there is no right or wrong answer because personal taste and preference play a big part. However, by adhering to these simple guidelines, you can improve your dining experience and discover new and exciting flavor combinations.

In the following chapter, we will look at the distinct qualities of Spanish sparkling wines and their ideal combinations with various types of cuisine.

## CHAPTER FIVE

## Rose Wines and Appetizer Pairings

Rosé wines have grown in popularity in recent years due to their refreshing and diverse nature. When it comes to producing high-quality rosé wines that match well with a range of appetizers, Spain is no exception. In this chapter, we'll look at some of Spain's best rosé wines and snack combinations.

### Pairings of Garnacha Rosé with Charcuterie

Garnacha Rosé is a pink wine created from the Garnacha grape varietal. It is also known as Grenache Rosé. It is well-known for its delicious flavors of strawberries, raspberries, and cherries, as well as its refreshing acidity. The acidity of the wine helps to cut through the rich and savory flavors of the cured meats, making Garnacha Rosé a perfect complement for charcuterie platters.

## Pairings of Cava Rosé and Seafood

Cava Rosé is a sparkling wine made from a combination of Spanish grape varietals including Macabeo, Parellada, and Xarello, as well as Pinot Noir. It is well-known for its delicate bubbles and red berry and citrus notes. Cava Rosé pairs well with seafood appetizers like shrimp cocktail or ceviche because the wine's acidity enhances the delicate tastes of the fish.

## Pairings of Rosado with Tapas

Rosado is a pink wine made from a combination of Spanish grapes including Tempranillo and Garnacha. It is well-known for its brilliant color and red fruit flavors such as strawberries and raspberries. Rosado pairs well with a range of tapas, such as patatas bravas or Spanish tortilla, because the wine's acidity and fruitiness compliment the dishes' robust and savory characteristics.

**Other Rosé Wines and Food Pairings**

There are several additional rosé wines that mix well with Spanish appetizers like Garnacha Rosé, Cava Rosé, and Rosado. For example, Tempranillo Rosé pairs well with cured meats and cheeses, but Bobal Rosé pairs well with spicy meals like chorizo.

**Rosé Wine Pairing Suggestions for Spanish Appetizers**

There are a few things to consider when matching rosé wines with Spanish appetizers.

**Consider the wine's acidity:** The acidity of the wine might influence how well it goes with food. Wines with high acidity, such as Garnacha Rosé and Cava Rosé, mix well with rich and savory appetizers, whilst wines with lower acidity, such as Rosado, fit well with lighter and more delicate appetizers.

**Consider the wine's sweetness:** Some rosés, like Moscato Rosé, can be quite sweet. When choosing a pairing, consider the sweetness of the wine, as it may dominate some appetizers.

**Experiment with different combinations:** Experiment with different rosé wines and appetizers to find new and unexpected flavor combinations, just as you would with other types of wine pairings.

Finally, rosé wines are a versatile and pleasant option that complement a wide range of Spanish appetizers. From charcuterie to seafood and tapas, there is rosé wine to complement your favorite cuisine. Consider the acidity and sweetness of the wine, as well as your personal taste preferences, when matching rosé wine with appetizers. You may find the perfect rosé wine and appetizer match to enjoy during your next wine and dine trip in Spain with a little experimentation.

## CHAPTER SIX

## Sherry and Tapas Pairings

Sherry is a distinct and adaptable wine produced in the Jerez region of southern Spain. It's a fortified wine, which means it's been fortified with distilled spirits, usually brandy, to raise the alcohol content. Sherry goes well with tapas, which are tiny dishes of savory snacks and appetizers beloved in Spain. In this chapter, we'll look at the many types of sherry and how they match with tapas.

### Pairings of Fino and Manzanilla Sherry

Fino and Manzanilla are two Sherries that are recognized for being dry and light-bodied. They are made from the Palomino grape and matured under a coating of yeast known as flor, which gives them a characteristic nutty and salty flavor. Fino and Manzanilla sherries go well with olives, almonds, and other salty foods because the salty flavor of the wine compliments the saltiness of the tapas.

## Sherry Pairings with Amontillado and Oloroso

Amontillado and Oloroso sherries are well-known for their rich, nutty flavor. They are made from the Palomino grape and are matured in contact with oxygen, giving them a deeper color and a more nuanced flavor. The wine's nutty and rich flavor matches the powerful flavors of the tapas. Amontillado and Oloroso sherry mix wonderfully with stronger-flavored tapas, such as spicy chorizo or blue cheese.

## Sherry Pairings with Pedro Ximenez

Pedro Ximenez is a sweet sherry made from the Pedro Ximenez grape variety. It's famous for its rich flavors of dried fruits including raisins and figs, as well as its syrupy texture. Pedro Ximenez sherry goes well with sweet tapas like chocolate or fruit desserts because the wine's sweetness balances the sweetness of the tapas.

**Sherry Pairing Suggestions for Tapas**

There are a few things to keep in mind when mixing sherry with tapas:

**Consider the sherry style:** The style of sherry can have an impact on how it interacts with meals. Dry and light-bodied sherries like Fino and Manzanilla match well with salty nibbles, whilst richer and nuttier sherries like Amontillado and Oloroso work well with robust and savory tapas.

**Consider the sherry's sweetness:** Sweet sherries, such as Pedro Ximenez, combine well with sweet tapas like sweets or fruit. They can also be used with salty snacks to create a distinct and contrasting flavor experience.

**Experiment with different combinations**: Experiment with different sherries and tapas to find new and intriguing flavor combinations, just as you would with other types of wine pairings.

Finally, sherry is a distinct and versatile wine that goes well with tapas. There is a sherry to complement the flavors of your favorite tapas, ranging from dry and light-bodied Fino and Manzanilla to rich and nutty Amontillado and Oloroso and sweet Pedro Ximenez. Consider the style and sweetness of the wine, as well as your personal taste preferences, when matching sherry with tapas. You may find the perfect sherry and tapas match to enjoy during your next wine and dine adventure in Spain with a little experimentation.

# CHAPTER SEVEN

## Cava and Cheese Pairings

Cava is a sparkling wine produced in Spain's Catalonia area. It's made the old-fashioned way, with a second fermentation in the bottle. Cava pairs well with cheese because its acidity and effervescence cut through the richness of the cheese, increasing its flavor. In this chapter, we'll look at the many types of cava and how they match with cheese.

## Champagne and Cava Pairings

The most popular style of cava is Brut cava, a dry sparkling wine. It tastes crisp and refreshing, with notes of green apple and citrus. Brut cava goes well with soft and creamy cheeses like brie and camembert, since the wine's acidity helps to temper the cheese's richness.

## Rosé and Cava Combinations

Rosé cava is a sparkling wine made in the same manner as Brut cava, but with a small amount of red wine added. It has a delicate and sweet flavor with strawberry and raspberry undertones. Rosé cava goes well with hard and nutty cheeses like aged gouda and cheddar, since the wine's fruity flavors enhance the cheese's nuttiness.

## Gran Reserva and Reserva Pairings for Cava

The minimum age for Reserva and Gran Reserva cava is 15 months and 30 months, respectively. They have a richer flavor profile, with roasted nuts and brioche flavors. Cava Reserva and Gran Reserva accompany blue cheeses like Roquefort and Gorgonzola because the wine's rich and toasted flavors match the pungent flavors of the cheese.

## Cava and Cheese Pairing Suggestions

There are a few things to bear in mind when mixing cava with cheese:

**Consider the cava style:** The style of cava can have an impact on how it mixes with cheese. Dry and crisp Brut cava complements soft and creamy cheeses, whereas fruity Rosé cava complements hard and nutty cheeses. Cava from the Reserva and Gran Reserva ages well with pungent and robust cheeses.

**Consider the cheese's spiciness:** The strength of the cheese can influence how well it goes with cava. Mild and creamy cheeses complement crisp and refreshing Brut cava, whilst robust and pungent cheeses complement rich and complex Reserva and Gran Reserva cava.

**Experiment with different combinations:** Experiment with various cava and cheese combos to discover new and fascinating flavor combinations.

Finally, cava is a versatile and delightful sparkling wine that goes well with cheese. There is a cava to complement the flavors of your favorite cheese, ranging from dry and crisp Brut cava to fruity Rosé cava and deep and complex Reserva and Gran Reserva cava. Consider the style and intensity of both the wine and the cheese when matching cava with cheese, and don't be hesitant to experiment with different combinations. You may find the perfect cava and cheese match to enjoy during your next wine and dine trip in Spain with a little experimentation.

# CHAPTER EIGHT

## Vermouth and Snack Pairings

Vermouth is a fortified wine flavored with herbs, spices, and, in some cases, fruits. It is a staple of Spanish cuisine and is widely consumed as an aperitif before meals. Vermouth has a rich and distinct flavor profile, with a bitter and sweet taste that pairs well with appetizers. This chapter will go over the many types of vermouth and their ideal pairings with appetizers.

### Pairings for Sweet Vermouth

The most common form of vermouth is sweet vermouth, which has a sweet and spicy flavor. It is commonly consumed on the rocks or in cocktails, but it also pairs well with appetizers. Sweet vermouth goes well with salty appetizers like olives, almonds, and potato chips. The vermouth's sweetness matches the saltiness of the appetizers, while the herbal notes in the vermouth aid to balance the flavors.

**Pairings with Dry Vermouth**

Dry vermouth is a less sweet vermouth with a more herbal and bitter flavor. It is frequently used in cocktails such as martinis, but it also goes well with appetizers. Dry vermouth complements savory appetizers like cured meats, pickled veggies, and cheese. The herbal and bitter tones in the vermouth match the rich tastes of the appetizers, while the vermouth's dryness aids in palate cleansing.

**Pairings for White Vermouth**

White vermouth, commonly known as blanc vermouth, is a fragrant and delicate vermouth. It is less frequent than sweet and dry vermouth, but it is still an excellent complement for appetizers. White vermouth goes well with light and refreshing appetizers like seafood, salads, and fresh fruit. The floral overtones in the vermouth complement the fresh flavors of the nibbles, while the sweetness balances the acidity.

## Vermouth Pairing Suggestions for Snacks

There are a few things to keep in mind when mixing vermouth with snacks:

**Consider the vermouth style:** The style of vermouth can influence how it mixes with food. Sweet vermouth complements salty snacks, dry vermouth complements savory snacks, and white vermouth complements light and fresh nibbles.

**Consider the snack's potency:** The strength of the snack can influence how well it goes with vermouth. Light and fresh snacks complement delicate and fragrant white vermouth, while salty and rich snacks complement sweet and spicy sweet vermouth. Herbal and bitter dry vermouth complements savory and rich appetizers best.

**Experiment with different combinations:** Experiment with various vermouth and snack combos to discover new and surprising flavor combinations.

Finally, vermouth is a delightful and adaptable fortified wine that pairs well with food. There is a vermouth to enhance the flavors of your favorite snacks, ranging from sweet and spicy sweet vermouth to herbal and bitter dry vermouth and delicate and floral white vermouth. Consider the style and intensity of both the wine and the food when pairing vermouth with snacks, and don't be hesitant to experiment with different combinations. You may find the perfect vermouth and snack pairing to enjoy during your next wine and dine trip in Spain with a little experimentation.

# CHAPTER NINE

## Dessert Wines and Sweet Pairings

Dessert wines are often sweet and rich, and they are ideal for matching with desserts or other sweet delicacies. There are many different types of dessert wines in Spain, each with its own distinct flavor profile and features. In this chapter, we will look at the various varieties of dessert wines available in Spain and their ideal matches with sweet sweets.

### Sherry

Sherry is a fortified wine from the Spanish area of Jerez. It is created from the Palomino grape that has been enhanced with brandy and matured in oak barrels. Sherry is available in a variety of varieties, from dry to sweet, and it goes well with a variety of sweets. Sweet sherries, such as Pedro Ximenez and Cream sherry, go well with chocolate treats like chocolate cake or chocolate truffles. The sherry's nutty and caramel aromas complement and enhance the richness of the chocolate.

**Moscatel** (Muscat) Moscatel is a sweet dessert wine created from the Muscat grape. It has a golden color, a honeyed scent, and a rich, fruity flavor. Moscatel goes well with sweet treats like fruit tarts or fruit salads. The wine's sweetness matches the natural sweetness of the fruit, while the wine's fruity undertones enhance the flavor of the dessert.

## Malaga

Malaga is a sweet dessert wine produced in Spain's Malaga region. It is created using sun-dried Pedro Ximenez and Moscatel grapes to concentrate their flavors. Malaga is a dark brown wine with a rich, sweet flavor. Malaga goes well with nutty desserts like almond cakes or pecan pies. The wine's nutty and caramel aromas match and accentuate the nuttiness of the dessert.

Suggestions for Matching Dessert Wines with Sweet Treats

There are a few things to keep in mind when matching dessert wines with sweet treats:

**Consider the level of sweetness:** When matching dessert wines with sweet sweets, the sweetness level of both the wine and the dessert must be considered. The wine should be sweeter than the dessert to ensure that it complements rather than overpowers the flavors.

**Take a look at the flavor profile:** The dessert wine's flavor profile should complement the flavors of the dessert. A fruity dessert wine like Moscatel, for example, goes well with fruit-based sweets, but a nutty dessert wine like Malaga goes well with nuts desserts.

**Experiment with different combinations:** Experiment with various dessert wine and sweet treat combos to discover new and fascinating flavor combinations.

Finally, dessert wines are a delectable and decadent way to cap a dinner in Spain. Dessert wines range from sweet and rich sherry to fruity and honeyed Moscatel and nutty and caramel Malaga. When matching dessert wines with sweet sweets, keep the sweetness level and flavor profile of both the wine and the dessert in mind. You may find the perfect dessert wine and sweet treat match to enjoy during your next wine and dine trip in Spain with a little experimentation.

# CHAPTER TEN

## Wine Tourism in Spain

With over 70 different wine regions and a long history of wine-making, Spain is one of the world's top wine-producing countries. In recent years, wine tourism has grown in popularity in Spain, with many wine fans travelling to the nation to enjoy its numerous superb wines and visit its scenic wine regions. We will look at wine tourism in Spain and what it has to offer in this chapter.

### Spain's Wine Regions

There are over 70 wine regions in Spain, each with its own distinct climate, grape varietals, and winemaking traditions. Some of Spain's most well-known wine areas include:

**Rioja:** Rioja, located in northern Spain, is possibly the most well-known wine area in the country, noted for its high-quality red wines made from the Tempranillo grape.

Ribera del Duero is a region in central Spain famed for its rich and robust red wines created from the Tempranillo grape.

**Priorat:** Priorat is a tiny wine region in Catalonia recognized for its high-quality red wines created from the Garnacha and Cariena grapes.

Jerez: Located in southern Spain, Jerez is famous for its one-of-a-kind fortified wine, sherry, manufactured from the Palomino vine.

**Penedes:** Located in Catalonia, Penedes is famed for its sparkling wine, cava, which is similar to champagne and is created in the traditional style.

**Spain Wine Tours**

Wine tours in Spain allow visitors to discover the country's numerous wine regions and drink its superb wines. Wine tours in Spain are provided in a variety of formats, including guided tours, self-directed tours, and private tours. Some of the most popular wine tours in Spain include: Rioja Wine Tours: Rioja is undoubtedly Spain's most famous wine area, and it is a popular wine tour destination. Visitors can visit the region's many wineries and experience its high-quality red wines.

**Ribera del Duero Wine Tours:** Another prominent wine region in Spain, Ribera del Duero is noted for its rich and robust red wines. Wine tours in Ribera del Duero allow tourists to experience the region's wineries and vineyards while learning about the region's winemaking traditions.

**Penedes Wine Tours:** Penedes is famous for its sparkling wine and cava, and wine tours in the region allow visitors to see the territory's vineyards and sample the region's many various types of cava.

**Jerez Wine Tours:** Jerez is famous for its fortified wine and sherry, and wine tours in the region allow visitors to learn about the winemaking process and experience the region's many distinct types of sherry.

## Museums and Exhibitions of Wine

Spain has numerous wine museums and exhibitions where visitors may learn more about the country's winemaking traditions and history. Some of Spain's most popular wine museums and exhibitions include:

**Vivanco Museum of Wine Culture:** The Vivanco Museum of Wine Culture, located in Rioja, is one of Spain's most prominent wine museums. The museum's exhibitions on the history of winemaking are complemented by a collection of wine-related items.

The Wine Museum of Malaga is set in a 16th-century castle in Malaga and has displays on the history of winemaking in the region.

**Wine Museum of Barcelona:** The Wine Museum of Barcelona, located in Barcelona, offers exhibitions on the history of winemaking in Catalonia, as well as a collection of wine-related items.

Finally, wine tourism in Spain provides a one-of-a-kind and memorable experience for those interested in learning about the country's rich wine culture. There is something for everyone among the over 70 wine areas, from the historic Rioja to the fashionable Priorat.

Visitors can take guided tours of wineries, vineyards, and tasting rooms to learn about the winemaking process and the region's history. Many wineries also provide food pairings and traditional Spanish cuisine, allowing you to enjoy both local meals and wines.

Many regions offer wine-themed activities such as grape stomping, wine and cheese pairings, and even hot air balloon rides over the vineyards in addition to traditional winery tours. Wine festivals, such as the renowned Haro Wine Festival in La Rioja, provide an opportunity to immerse oneself in the best of Spanish wine culture.

Spain's wine tourism business has grown significantly in recent years, and the country is now one of the world's top wine tourist destinations. This is due, in part, to the high quality of its wines, but it is also owing to the variety of experiences accessible to visitors.

Overall, wine tourism in Spain is a fantastic way to learn about Spanish culture, experience delectable wines and cuisine, and make lifelong memories. A wine tour in Spain is not to be missed if you are a wine connoisseur or simply searching for a unique travel experience. Wine Tourism in Spain

## CHAPTER ELEVEN

## Spanish Wine and Food Festivals

Spain is well-known for its bright and energetic culture, which is especially evident at wine and cuisine festivals. Many festivals are held throughout the year to celebrate the country's rich culinary heritage and world-renowned wines.

The La Batalla del Vino, or Wine Battle, is one of Spain's most famous wine festivals, held in the Rioja region's town of Haro. This festival commemorates Saint Peter's Day by showering participants in red wine with squirt guns, buckets, and any other means available. It is a vibrant and one-of-a-kind event that draws guests from all over the world.

The Festa del Vi, held in the village of Falset in the Priorat area, is another notable wine festival in Spain. This festival honors the region's wine, which is recognized for its robust, intense flavor. Wine tastings, food pairings, and other cultural events, such as traditional Catalan dancing, are available to visitors.

The Festa del Marisco in Galicia is a must-see for seafood enthusiasts. This festival honors the region's rich seafood culture with foods including octopus, mussels, and crab. These meals can be sampled while drinking local wines and listening to traditional Galician music.

Spain also features a number of wine festivals, such as the Fiesta de la Vendimia in Jerez, which commemorates the sherry harvest. Visitors to this festival can partake in grape stomping, tastings, and other sherry-related activities.

In addition to wine festivals, Spain hosts numerous food festivals that highlight the country's rich cuisine. For example, the Feria de Abril in Seville is a large celebration of Andalusian culture that includes traditional meals like gazpacho and paella. Another prominent festival is the San Sebastian Gastronomika, which brings together some of the world's greatest chefs for a week of cooking demonstrations, tastings, and workshops.

Overall, wine and food festivals in Spain are a fantastic chance to learn about the country's rich culinary tradition and world-renowned wines. These festivals are not to be missed if you are a wine connoisseur or simply searching for a unique cultural experience.

# CHAPTER TWELVE

## Conclusion and Final Thoughts

Exploring the wide world of Spanish cuisine and wine reveals that there is something for everyone. Spain's gastronomic choices are large and varied, ranging from fresh seafood and crisp white wines on the coast to strong meat dishes and rich red wines in the interior.

The emphasis on simple, high-quality ingredients is one of the distinctive elements of Spanish cuisine. The flavors are always fresh and vivid, whether it's a platter of fresh tomatoes drizzled with olive oil or a grilled octopus tentacle seasoned with just a touch of paprika.

When it comes to wine, Spain's wine regions have something for everyone. There is a wine for every occasion, from the crisp and refreshing Cava to the rich and complex Rioja. There are also many intriguing new wines to discover with the rise of natural and biodynamic winemaking processes.

Spanish food and wine matching is an art form in and of itself, and there are many traditional pairings that work well together. However, experimenting with different combinations to find what works best for your own palate is also recommended.

There are various resources available for individuals interested in learning more about Spanish cuisine and wine, including cookbooks, wine guides, and internet resources. Furthermore, wine and food tourism in Spain provides a unique opportunity to immerse oneself in the culture and cuisine.

Finally, Spanish cuisine and wine are diverse, rich, and endlessly fascinating. There is always something new to discover in this vibrant and rich cuisine, whether you are a seasoned wine connoisseur or an inquisitive eater. So pour yourself a glass of your favorite Spanish wine and enjoy the aromas of this unique culinary tradition. Salud!